THE LIBRARY OF
AMERICAN
LIVES AND TIMES™

PATRICK HENRY

Voice of the Revolution

Amy Kukla
Jon Kukla

The Rosen Publishing Group's
PowerPlus Books™
New York

*For Mark Condon and E. E. Fleming,
excellent high-school history teachers*

Published in 2002 by The Rosen Publishing Group, Inc.
29 East 21st Street, New York, NY 10010

First Edition

*Editor's Note: All quotations have been reproduced as they appeared in
the letters and diaries they were borrowed from. No correction was
made to the inconsistent spelling that was common in that time period.*

Library of Congress Cataloging-in-Publication Data
Kukla, Amy.
   Patrick Henry : voice of the Revolution / Amy Kukla and Jon
Kukla.—1st ed.
      p. cm. —(The library of American lives and times)
Includes bibliographical references and index.
   ISBN 0–8239–5725–X
   1. Henry, Patrick, 1736–1799—Juvenile literature. 2. Legislators—
United States—Biography—Juvenile literature. 3. United States.
Continental Congress—Biography—Juvenile literature. 4. Virginia—
Politics and government—1775–1783—Juvenile literature. 5. United
States—Politics and government—1775–1783—Juvenile literature. [1.
Henry, Patrick, 1736–1799. 2. Legislators. 3. United States—Politics
and government—1775–1783.] I. Kukla, Jon, 1948– II. Title. III.
Series.
   E302.6.H5 K85 2002
   973.3'092—dc21
                                                    00–012005

Manufactured in the United States of America

CONTENTS

1. Making of a Leader

Virginia was larger when Patrick Henry was alive than it is today. Before the American Revolution, Virginia extended west from the Atlantic Ocean all the way to the Mississippi River, and from North Carolina all the way to the Great Lakes. When Patrick Henry was born, Virginia had about 150,000 residents. Rich or poor, free or slave, most Virginians lived on farms or plantations and grew food for themselves and tobacco to sell in England and Europe. Most of the population lived near tributaries of the James, York, Rappahannock, and Potomac Rivers, which were deep enough for the largest sailing ships of the eighteenth century. The Atlantic Ocean linked Virginians to the markets of Europe and to their king. Virginians were proud to be Great Britain's oldest and largest royal colony in America, and they cherished their rights under English law and government.

This portrait of Patrick Henry is by David Silvette. It was created from the well-known portrait by Thomas Sully, which was painted after Henry's death. The painting is on display at Red Hill, Patrick Henry's last home and burial place.

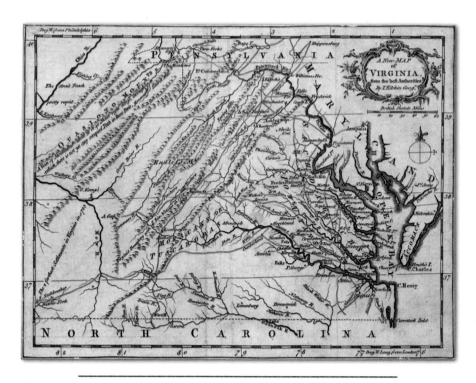

This map of Virginia by T. Kitchin was created in the 1700s. The York River is in the lower right of the map, the second large river from the bottom, off Chesapeake Bay. The South Anna River, where Patrick Henry canoed with his cousins, is located toward the center, just to the east of the first line of mountains.

Things were about to change, though, and Patrick Henry would be at the forefront of the action. So, who was this Patrick Henry who later would be known as the Voice of the Revolution? His story begins in the 1700s at a place called Studley.

● ● ● ● ● ●

White dogwood blossoms peeked out through the green and brown trees near the house named Studley. The house stood in the middle of the forest near Totopotomoy Creek, a tributary of the wide York River.

John Syme, married to Sarah Winston Syme, built Studley on a tobacco plantation in Hanover County, Virginia. They had one child before John Syme's death made Sarah a widow.

Sarah married John Henry a few years later. He was a college-educated farmer and surveyor who came to Virginia from Scotland. They had eleven children together, but two died at young ages. William, Patrick, and nine younger sisters all were born at Studley. The Henrys welcomed Patrick into their family on May 29, 1736. He spent the first fourteen years of his life there.

Patrick Henry attended school for a few years. He learned the basic skills of reading, writing, and arithmetic. Then his family moved west to Mount Brilliant, a more isolated part of Hanover County. His father decided to educate his children at home. John Henry had studied at King's College of Aberdeen University in Scotland. So had his brother, who earned a Master of Arts and was ordained in the Scottish Episcopal Church. Patrick Henry's father did most of the teaching, although his uncle may have tutored young Patrick in Greek, Latin, and religion.

This is the late fifteenth-century university building of the city of Aberdeen in the Grampian region of Scotland.

Patrick Henry's favorite subject was mathematics,

but he enjoyed reading, too. Above all, he enjoyed the study of nature itself. Patrick Henry was much happier in the woods hunting or fishing than with his schoolbooks. He spent as much time as he could walking barefoot through the Virginia countryside.

Friends often found him "lying under the shade of some tree . . . watching for hours, at the same spot, the motionless cork of his fishing line." He was observant, always aware of the things that were happening around him. This trait was important for a hunter. It also would be useful when he became a lawyer and a politician. Constant observations of daily life in Virginia taught Henry what the citizens needed from their lawmakers. Patrick Henry enjoyed being with people at work, at the market, at church, or in court. He became one of the most popular politicians in America.

The great patriot led a simple childhood. He was educated by his father and spent the rest of his time hunting and fishing in the woods, and playing with friends. His friends remembered that young Patrick Henry seemed careless about his outward appearance, but particular about personal hygiene and clean linens.

A cousin remembered his playful side, too. Henry often overturned their canoe and threw his cousins, fully dressed, into the South Anna River. His cousins would come to the surface and find Henry giggling at his prank. In time they realized that "under some pretense or other," Patrick Henry always removed his clothes before tipping the canoe.

Patrick Henry's violin, pictured here, is on display at Red Hill, in Brookneal, Virginia.

Music was important to Patrick Henry and Virginians of his day. He learned to play the violin quite skillfully. Henry's fiddling entertained family and friends until the last months of his life. When Henry was about twelve years old, he broke his collarbone and was confined to bed. To fight boredom, he taught himself to play the flute. Close friends said he could play the flute well. Not many people ever heard him play it, however, because he preferred to entertain his family and friends with his violin.

As a young boy, Patrick Henry developed a strong religious faith. He was baptized in the Church of England, where his father worshiped. The Church of England, or Anglican church, was the established church in colonial Virginia. Hanover County also had Presbyterian churches and Quaker meetings that were not supported by taxes, or tithes. Henry's mother, Sarah, often brought him along when she attended Presbyterian services.

While Patrick Henry was young, America was

This portrait of Samuel Davies, by an unknown artist, seems to be based on a portrait by Alexander Von Jost that hangs in the Hanover Courthouse. The Reverend Samuel Davies was born in Summit Ridge, Delaware. He was sent to Virginia in 1747, as an Evangelist, and he founded five churches, three which are still in existence.

*Patrick Henry left
behind so few letters, journals,
or recorded speeches that the story
of his life has to be gathered from what
his friends and enemies had to say about
him. In fact, even for most of his famous
speeches we are forced to rely on people
who were inspired enough to want
to remember and record
his words.*

experiencing a religious movement called the Great Awakening, a spiritual revival. Ministers preached animated and passionate sermons about how sinful the colonists had become. These were the services Patrick Henry attended with his mother. On the way home, she quizzed him about the sermon they had just heard. Eventually, Patrick Henry learned to repeat entire sermons for his mother in the dramatic style of the dissenting ministers. One of the best of these preachers was Samuel Davies, who later became president of the Presbyterian college in Princeton, New Jersey. Samuel Davies had a strong influence on the oratorical style of

Patrick Henry. People called Patrick Henry the "son of thunder" because his speeches later in life had the passion and drama he learned from revival sermons.

Patrick Henry's faith and morals, developed in his youth, shaped his daily behavior as an adult. He knew that vigorous debate was more effective when he refrained from "strong language." Friends and colleagues remarked that he never swore or used curse words to emphasize his opinions. Unlike some politicians and plantation owners of his day, Patrick Henry did not gamble. He was strongly committed to his wife and 17 children, and his personal life was never the object of gossip. In the inns and taverns of colonial Virginia, Patrick Henry was known as a man everyone liked. After the Revolution, he saw many of his countrymen ruining their lives with whiskey. He tried to reduce the use of distilled liquors by encouraging people to drink beer. In his private life and in politics, Patrick Henry cherished his faith and lived by its values.

2. Farmer, Storekeeper, and Lawyer

Wealthy Virginia planters often sent their sons to college when they were about 15, but John Henry could not afford that. When Patrick Henry was 15, he worked as a store clerk for about a year. Then, in 1752, John Henry opened a store of his own that Patrick and his brother William managed. Both brothers were equally responsible, but William lacked interest and stayed away. Patrick shouldered most of the work, but the business suffered when the young boys sold too many things on credit to customers who did not pay their bills. Within a year, their store went broke and had to be closed.

In the fall of 1754, 18-year-old Patrick Henry married Sarah Shelton, who lived near Studley and whose grandfather published the *Virginia Gazette*. Sarah's father gave the couple a 600-acre (243 ha) tobacco farm named Pine Slash, its house, and six slaves. Patrick and Sarah Henry lived at Pine Slash for about three years while Patrick tried his luck at farming. Times were hard in Virginia: "Money is scarcer than it has been for many years," wrote one of Patrick Henry's neighbors. "Our spring crops of wheat and barley,

This 1877 etching by Alonzo Chapell shows Edward Braddock, who lived from 1695 to 1755. He was a Scottish soldier in command of British forces in America during the French and Indian War. He was wounded and died on his way to attack Fort Dusquesne on July 9, 1755.

oats and rye have been ruined by an early drought." Farms suffered everywhere in the colony, and to make matters worse the French and Indian War had begun between France and Great Britain. Nevertheless, Patrick and Sarah Henry soon had their first child in 1755, a daughter they named Martha.

Then came tragedy. Patrick Henry's attempt at farming came to an end in 1757. Fire destroyed the young couple's home and possessions. They moved into a small cabin, sold their slaves, and used the money to open a store. Still, the drought ravaged Virginia. Crops died, farms failed, and so did Patrick Henry's second store. Only his family grew. Patrick and Sarah welcomed the birth of their son John in 1757.

Fortunately, Sarah's father owned the tavern across the street from Hanover Courthouse. About 1760, Patrick, Sarah, and their growing family moved into Hanover Tavern. While there, Patrick Henry helped Sarah's father with the business at the bar. Lawyers from the courthouse across the street often came to the tavern to talk about their cases after a day at the courts. Patrick Henry listened to their conversations and learned the details of their profession. In his spare time, Patrick read law books or observed sessions of the county court.

Hanover Courthouse was built in 1735. Made of brick, it is one of the best examples in the nation of an arched form of architecture called neoclassical, which was popular in colonial times.

Patrick Henry had spent less than a year reading law and observing the judicial system in action when he rode to Williamsburg, the capital of colonial Virginia, to get his law license. To practice law in Virginia, Henry had to pass a test given by four of the colony's most

The Colonial Capitol Building in Williamsburg, Virginia, originally was built by a contractor named Henry Cary. It burned down twice and was reconstructed each time with slight modifications. It is in this building that Patrick Henry made his famous Caesar-Brutus speech.

prominent lawyers. All four examiners advised Patrick Henry to continue studying the law, but they signed his license, saying, "they perceived him to be a young man of genius and did not doubt he would soon qualify himself." Patrick Henry returned to Hanover County where he opened a small law practice. At first he handled small civil cases, often lawsuits to collect debts. There were still many weeks when Patrick Henry had time for hunting, fishing, and spending time outdoors. During this time, Patrick and Sarah Henry also welcomed another addition to their family, William, born in 1763.

The courts of Virginia heard important cases four times a year. At each quarterly session, citizens from Hanover and the surrounding counties gathered at the courthouse to hear the colony's best lawyers in action. During the December session in 1763, people came to hear the final arguments in The Parson's Cause. Tobacco was the main crop in the colonies near Chesapeake Bay. Year after year, the farmers of Virginia and Maryland grew so much of it that the prices stayed low, less than two cents per pound, and seldom changed. They paid their bills with tobacco. They sold it to England and Europe to pay for imported clothing, tools, books, wine, and other European products. They even paid their taxes with tobacco, including the taxes that supported the established church and its ministers.

This is a drawing of a tobacco plant, the main crop of Virginia and Maryland.

The same droughts that had ruined Patrick Henry's farm and his store also reduced the amount of tobacco that farmers brought to market. The scarcity of tobacco drove the prices much higher than normal, making each pound of tobacco worth much more than in years past. If everyone else was suffering from the bad harvest,

This eighteenth-century painting of King George III was created by Thomas Gainsborough. George III was born in 1738. He ruled Britain during the American Revolution and wished to keep the colonies under control. George had a disease called porphyria, which caused madness. In 1811, during the last years of his reign, rule was given to his son. George III died blind, deaf, and mad at Windsor Castle on January 29, 1820.

would it be fair if the ministers received extra pay just because tobacco was scarce? The burgesses, or lawmakers, in Virginia said no. They passed a law called the Two-Penny Act, so that ministers would be paid in currency equal to the value of the tobacco they were paid each year before the drought.

Although Virginians believed that their rights as Englishmen empowered them to decide how much the people had to pay in taxes, some of the Anglican ministers complained to King George III and his advisers in England. They wanted to be paid at the current market value of tobacco, not the old price. At this time, there was no separation between Church and State. In fact, the Church

Parishes of the established church in Virginia reported to the Bishop of London, who was too busy to worry about some colonial parsons who felt they were being underpaid. The Two-Penny Act made the parsons angry, as they too were feeling the effects of the drought and financial hardships of that time. They tried several times to appeal the legislation, but failed. Going over the Virginian lawmakers' heads to the king was a big mistake, however. Not only was all of Hanover County suffering financially, they felt it was their right to make laws to govern themselves. This problem would crop up again and again, and eventually it would spark a revolution.

was extremely powerful in matters of government and most people did not question its authority. The parsons won the first part of their case because the king had decided that the Two-Penny Act was illegal. The lawyer who lost the case gave up and resigned. His resignation gave Henry an important opportunity.

The vestry, or church council, hired Patrick Henry to persuade the jury not to pay the parsons the full amount of money they wanted. When Patrick Henry delivered his first public speech in the courtroom of Hanover County, he became a hero to the common citizens of Virginia. At last Patrick Henry had found his calling as a lawyer and a courageous voice for political and religious liberty.

3. The Parsons' Cause: "Enemies of the Community"

Patrick Henry Jr. ran along the dirt road in Hanover County, Virginia, one cold December day in 1763. He was hurrying to meet his uncle's carriage. The young lawyer had been named for his uncle, the Reverend Patrick Henry, who was an Anglican parson in the Church of England. This was an important day for young Patrick Henry. The parish vestry, or council, of a local church had hired him to represent it in court. It quickly became an important day in American history.

The court had decided the parish owed money to its parson. Now the jury had to decide how much. Patrick Henry was running because he knew he had harsh things to say about Virginia's clergy and he wanted to warn his uncle. Nearly out of breath, Patrick caught his

This pullout from the Cooke painting (page 23) shows John Henry, Patrick's father. The artist portrays him with a handkerchief because he was supposedly moved to tears by his son's words.

uncle's carriage near the courthouse. He jumped to the door, and asked him not to come to court. He did not want Reverend Henry to feel offended.

It was only natural that a proud uncle would come to hear his nephew argue his first big case. If only the case had been about a stolen horse or disputed property line, anything but another minister's salary. As they talked on that winter day in 1763, both men knew that The Parsons' Cause was really about bigger political issues. The Reverend Patrick Henry told his driver to turn the carriage around, and he headed home.

Patrick Henry entered the small, brick courthouse. It was full of spectators. Patrick looked up to see the judges. His father, John Henry, was the presiding judge. Would Patrick make his father proud that day? Would justice be done? Patrick Henry was nervous as he got ready to speak to the judges and the jury.

All eyes in the courtroom were on him as Patrick Henry rose to his feet. All ears strained to hear what he would say. He started slowly. He could not look at his father. His voice faltered. He had trouble finding the right words. His father looked away, disappointed by his son's awkward start. The other judges were puzzled, wondering where his speech was going. It seemed without focus.

Slowly, Patrick Henry found his words, and his voice. He began to speak with confidence. His voice grew full and strong. He provoked the jury to anger at the thought of parsons suing their parishioners for more money. "We

This painting showing Patrick Henry arguing The Parsons' Cause is credited to George Cooke and was painted about 1830. Notice the positioning of the map of Virginia in the center, and the worried faces on the men listening to Henry's words. This was one of the first instances where the issue of the colonists' right to a voice in the government became prominent.

have heard a great deal about the benevolence and holy zeal of our reverend clergy," he said. "Do they practice the mild and benevolent precepts of the Gospel of Jesus? Do they feed the hungry and clothe the naked? Oh, no," Patrick Henry complained. "Instead of feeding the hungry and clothing the naked," the greedy parsons would "snatch from the hearth of their honest parishioner his last hoe-cake, from the widow and her orphan children their last milk cow! The last bed, nay, the last blanket!"

As his excitement increased Patrick Henry pushed

> By the time
> Patrick Henry was assigned
> to The Parsons' Cause, he
> was 27 years old. Far from being
> inexperienced, he had been practicing
> law for four years and had already tried
> 493 cases in 1763. He charged just
> 15 shillings for his work in what
> would become his most
> famous case.

his glasses up onto his forehead. He spoke for almost an hour. "The Established Church and Clergy," he said, had responsibilities in society. "When a Clergy ceases to answer these ends, the community . . . may justly strip them of their appointments." He regretted that the ministers were acting like "enemies of the community." He was outraged that King George III had taken their side.

Good government, Patrick Henry said, depended on "the original compact between king and people." The king offered "protection on one hand." The people responded with "obedience on the other." The farmers of Virginia were suffering from bad harvests. Their elected representatives, called burgesses, had passed a law in 1758 adjusting the church taxes until the next good harvest ended the economic crisis. Except for a few parsons, Henry said, everyone in Virginia agreed "that the act of 1758 had every characteristic of a good law. It was a law of general utility." The parsons, however, complained to King George III across the Atlantic Ocean, and his advisers overruled the Virginia law.

The sound of Patrick Henry's voice filled the tiny courtroom. The judges, the jury, and the spectators were amazed. If a king overruled "acts of this salutary nature," Henry thundered, he became "a tyrant and forfeits all right to his subjects' obedience!"

A few spectators cried out "Treason, Treason!" The parson's attorney complained to the judges "that the gentleman had spoken treason." They were too late. Patrick Henry's fiery speech worked. The jury deliberated for five minutes and came back with a verdict. They rewarded the parson only one farthing, about the equivalent of today's penny, in back pay.

When they heard the verdict, the citizens of Hanover County treated Henry as a hero. They lifted him on their shoulders and shouted cheers of joy. Word of his moving speech traveled rapidly. Patrick Henry quickly became a hero for people far beyond Hanover County. The case came to be called The Parsons' Cause. Soon Patrick Henry's reputation for eloquence began to grow throughout the colony.

4. "If This Be Treason"

Virginians believed that they were Englishmen entitled to all the rights of Englishmen. Ever since they started their colony on Jamestown Island in 1607, they had lived under English law. For more than 150 years, they enjoyed its guarantees of free speech, free press, trial by jury, and the right to tax themselves. The king and his advisers sent an Englishman to be their royal governor. The king also appointed important colonial planters to the Council, which shared executive power with the governor. These councilors also served as the General Court, Virginia's highest judicial body. The citizens of each county in Virginia, however, elected their own lawmakers, called burgesses. Like members of the English Parliament, the burgesses met in the capitol at Williamsburg nearly every year. They passed laws for the colony, and they decided what taxes would be collected. The House of Burgesses was the lower house of the General Assembly, but it became very important in the mid-eighteenth century. After two years of practicing law, Patrick Henry was elected to the Virginia House of Burgesses in 1765.

This 1851 painting by Peter F. Rothermel is titled *Patrick Henry Before the Virginia House of Burgesses*. He is presenting his resolutions against the Stamp Act. The fifth resolution was the American colonies' first open declaration of independence from parliamentary taxation.

Patrick Henry took his office as a burgess for Louisa County, just west of Hanover, on May 20, 1765. His first few days as a burgess were not very exciting. The burgesses discussed routine things, like stopping pigs from running in the streets of the new town of Richmond. They tried to avoid talking about the Stamp Act.

From 1754 in North America (and from 1756 in Europe and India), Great Britain and its allies had fought France and its allies in a war that ended in 1763. Americans call it the French and Indian War. Europeans call it the Seven Years' War. It was the first worldwide imperial war in modern history. The English won, but winning was expensive. England was left with a huge debt. The British Parliament, which made British laws, decided to collect taxes from the colonies to help pay for the war. In 1764, Parliament placed a tax on all printed material in the colonies. They called it the Stamp Act. The act required a tax stamp on all printed things and official docu-ments. Tax stamps, like those on tobacco and alcohol products in many states today, were used to show that the Stamp Tax had been paid. This Stamp Act would raise the prices of newspa-pers, legal documents, and even playing cards. Like The

This is one of the stamps attached by the British to goods sold in the American colonies once the Stamp Act was passed.

Parsons' Cause, however, there was a bigger issue, too. The colonists had never before been taxed in this way. They believed that their rights as Englishmen empowered them to decide for themselves, through their colonial legislatures, how much to pay in taxes. The colonists had no voice or representation in Parliament. If Parliament legally could make them pay the Stamp Tax, what would happen to their rights?

As the end of May approached, some burgesses began to leave so they could get back home and tend their crops. Patrick Henry watched with alarm as experienced lawmakers reacted timidly to the Stamp Act. The older burgesses were trying to object to the Stamp Act without speaking out strongly against the king of England. Patrick Henry thought these men were too timid. If someone did not speak against the Stamp Act, it meant that Parliament would gain primary control over the finances of the colonies.

Patrick Henry quickly wrote down five resolutions about the Stamp Act on a blank sheet of an old law book. He then showed them to two other frontier burgesses, John Fleming of Cumberland County and George Johnston of Fairfax County. These two men encouraged Patrick Henry to propose his resolutions. They promised their support. In fact, Fleming and Johnston drew up two more resolutions, even more critical of the Stamp Act, to be presented if Henry's first five resolutions passed the House.

This is a portrait of George Johnston who, along with John Fleming, added two more resolutions to Henry's five. Though the resolutions were never presented to the burgesses they were widely reprinted throughout the colonies.

On May 29, 1765, his twenty-ninth birthday, Patrick Henry entered the House of Burgesses to present his resolutions against the Stamp Act. He had been a member of the House of Burgesses for only eight days, but he was already becoming known as a great orator and rising leader in the House. The burgesses passed a few minor business details before attending to the important subject of the day. Patrick Henry read his five resolutions and George Johnston seconded them. Each resolution detailed one of the colonists'

This is Oliver Cromwell, to whom Patrick Henry referred in his speech. He forcibly took control of England from Charles I.

objections to the Stamp Act, but it was the fifth resolution that caused great debate. The fifth resolution declared that only the General Assembly of Virginia had the right and power to impose taxes on the citizens of the colony. If this fifth resolution passed, it would, in essence, deny British Parliament the power to tax the colonists of Virginia in any manner. This fifth resolution, though short and simple, was the colonists' first declaration of independence from parliamentary taxation.

A heated debate began. Then Patrick Henry rose to defend his resolutions with a daring speech. Referring to past tyrants who had been assassinated or executed, Patrick Henry stated passionately: "Caesar had his Brutus, Charles the First his Cromwell, and George the Third . . ." Patrick Henry paused after speaking the name of the king of England, George III, in his list of rulers who had been killed by those they governed. While he paused, shouts of treason were heard around the room. The echoes fell quiet. Patrick Henry finished his sentence: "and George the Third . . . may profit by their example. If this be treason, make the most of it." The vote was taken and each of the five resolutions passed, though by slim margins. Patrick Henry's fifth resolution passed by just one vote—20 to 19. It called the Stamp Act a threat that would destroy British as well as American freedom.

Patrick Henry's speech against the Stamp Act, The Caesar-Brutus Speech, established his reputation as one of history's greatest orators. Virginia's royal governor thought differently. "In the course of debates," he reported to British officials, "very indecent language was used by a Mr. Henry, a young lawyer." A fellow burgess thought "Mr. Henry's manly eloquence surpassed everything of the kind I had ever heard before." Years later, a young college student who had been listening from the doorway on that historic day would express his opinion, too. Patrick Henry, said future president Thomas Jefferson, "appeared to me to speak as Homer wrote."

5. Lighting the Flame of the Revolution

The vote in the House of Burgesses had been very close. After Patrick Henry and many other burgesses went home, his opponents were able to reconsider and defeat the fifth and strongest resolution. Soon it did not matter whether the House of Burgesses changed its vote. Copies of all five resolutions, plus the additional resolutions by John Fleming and George Johnston, were sent to the other colonies and published in newspapers. Patrick Henry's resolutions inspired patriots in all the colonies from Massachusetts to Georgia. Patrick Henry and the burgesses of Virginia had taken a giant step toward declaring full and complete independence from Great Britain.

Eventually the British Parliament repealed the Stamp Act. They replaced it with a Declaratory Act, which claimed power over the colonies in all things, including the imposition of taxes. The situation remained tense for several years until Parliament placed a tax on tea. The issues remained the same but this was the final straw. In December

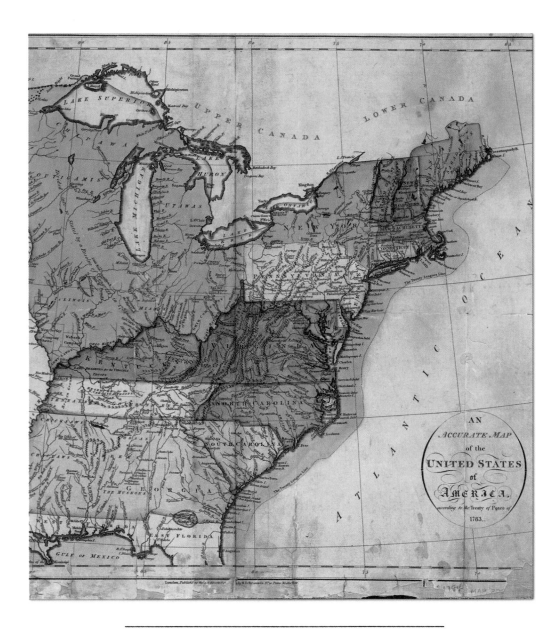

This map was created in 1783 after the Treaty of Paris, ending the Revolutionary War that officially began in 1775. It shows the thirteen states in the United States of America. It is an important map because it is one of the first made after America gained its independence from Britain.

This 1856 color engraving, created by John Andrew, shows the Boston Tea Party of December 16, 1773. The men in the boat were patriots dressed as Mohawk Indians. In protest against a tax on tea, they threw 342 chests of tea into the harbor, while citizens in Boston cheered them on. The British punished the colonists with the Coercive, or Intolerable, Acts.

1773, a group of patriots disguised as Native Americans threw a cargo of British East India Company tea into the Boston Harbor rather than allowing the tea to be sold and the tax collected. This act of defiance became known as the Boston Tea Party. Parliament sent troops to punish the city of Boston, close its port, and force the colonists to submit. News traveled quickly to Virginia. The burgesses held a day of fasting and prayer for

American freedom. They also agreed, with the other colonies, to send delegates to Philadelphia to begin working together. "The flame is spread through all the continent," Virginia's royal governor warned, "and one colony supports another in their disobedience to superior powers." Patrick Henry's resolutions against the Stamp Act lit the match.

6. Sadness at Home

About 1771, Patrick Henry bought a fine house named Scotchtown in Hanover County. He hoped it would be a pleasant home for Sarah. She had given birth to three more children, Anne, Betsey, and Edward. After Edward was born, Sarah's mental health began to decline. As insanity claimed her mind, Sarah became unable to care for herself or her family. The colony had just opened a lunatic asylum in Williamsburg, but its facilities were more like a prison than a hospital. At Scotchtown she could live out her life at home in the care of people who loved her. "One of the airy, sunny rooms in the half-basement" was made into a secure and comfortable living space. Sarah never regained her sanity, and she died at Scotchtown in 1775.

Scotchtown was built around 1719 by Charles Chiswell. It is one of the oldest surviving plantation houses in Virginia. Patrick Henry and his family lived there from 1771 to 1778.

Patrick Henry's "soul was bowed down . . . under the

heaviest sorrows and personal distresses." To deal with his grief, Patrick Henry focused his energy on the important process of encouraging unity with the other colonies. In 1774, Virginia sent him to Philadelphia with George Washington and other leaders for the First Continental Congress. During this meeting, the colonies developed a non-importation association that put pressure on British merchants by refusing to import British goods.

This portrait of John Adams was painted between 1796-1800. Adams would be the second U.S. president.

The delegates hoped their boycott would force Parliament to stop taxing the colonists without their consent. Again they were disappointed. Parliament sent troops to New England and New York.

At the First Continental Congress, in 1774, Patrick Henry met patriots from the other colonies for the first time. During this meeting, he said, "The distinctions between Virginians, Pennsylvanians, New Yorkers, and New Englanders, are no more. I am not a Virginian, but an American." Meeting together in the Continental Congress, the colonies took an important step toward independence. Many delegates were reluctant to speak of separation from England. Massachusetts patriot John Adams said only Patrick Henry "appeared to me sensible of the precipice . . . on which he stood, and had candor and courage enough to acknowledge it."

7. "We Must Fight"

In March 1775, the Second Virginia Convention was held at St. John's Church in Richmond, Virginia. Virginians wanted to meet and decide what to do about the situation that was developing. They could not meet in the capitol in Williamsburg, where they would be watched by the governor, so they decided to meet in a small village about 60 miles (96.6 km) to the west instead. High above the James River, the Second Virginia Convention gathered in the largest building in Richmond, the parish church, now known as St. John's Church.

The people of Virginia held five Revolutionary Conventions from 1774 to 1776. Each one followed the familiar rules of the House of Burgesses—except that they called the presiding officer president instead of speaker. The

St. John's Church, in Richmond, Virginia, was built in 1741, on land donated by William Byrd II. This church is the site where Patrick Henry gave his famous Liberty or Death speech.

Most of the colonies formed Committees of Safety to help govern the colonies as well as manage the militia. The Virginia Convention appointed a Committee of Safety of 11 members on August 16. The Committee's purpose was to make sure all ordinances and resolutions of the Convention were carried out, and to commission military officers and provide for the troops, including salaries and other expenses. It was also in charge of war supplies.

The Committee also was made commander in chief of the army. If danger threatened the colony and the troops that the Convention had commissioned could not be ready, the Committee could call on the existing militia.

conventions claimed their power to govern from the people of Virginia, not from the king. They no longer obeyed the royal governor, and a small group of elected leaders, called the Committee of Safety, ran the government between conventions.

On March 23, the Convention began with a prayer asking God to protect King George III and guide him toward better policies. The delegates approved the minutes of the previous convention and voted to send thanks to Jamaica for supporting the colonies' position against England. Patrick Henry stood to present a series of resolutions. He proposed that Virginia call out the militia, the forerunner of the U. S. National Guard, and get ready to defend the

This is an engraving by H.B. Hall of Patrick Henry addressing the Second Virginia Revolutionary Committee. It was during this meeting that Patrick would deliver his famous Liberty or Death speech urging Virginia to prepare for war. Notice that the Stamp Act, which had sparked some of the earliest protests against the king, lies crumpled on the floor.

colony should the British attempt to force them into submission. Colonel George Washington, Thomas Jefferson, and about half the delegates agreed that the colony should prepare to defend itself. Other patriot leaders opposed Patrick Henry's resolutions because they still hoped for peace with Great Britain. The Americans had some friends in Parliament, they argued, who might change the king's policies if they were given more time. George Washington, who was the most respected soldier in Virginia, rose and said he would rather prepare for the worst. He offered to pay for a company of militia himself.

George Washington. Esq.
Americanischer Generalissimus.

This engraving of George Washington shows him as an American general. Washington was commander in chief of the Continental army and became the first president of the United States of America.

This 1915 painting by Clyde D. DeLand shows Patrick Henry passionately giving his Liberty or Death speech. DeLand was still trying to capture the excitement and importance of this moment in history 140 years after Henry gave his speech.

As Washington took his seat, Patrick Henry rose and asked permission to address the convention.

As Patrick Henry began the most famous speech of his career, he admitted that the American colonies

There were many men who disagreed with Patrick Henry's wish to rise up against England. These men were afraid to start a war they were not sure they could win. Edmund Pendleton, of Caroline County, said: "We must arm, you say; but gentlemen must remember that blows are apt to follow the arming, and blood will follow blows, and, sir, when this occurs the dogs of war will be loosed, friends will be converted into enemies, and this flourishing country will be swept with a tornado of death and destruction." He was urging the colonists to use caution and to think carefully before leaping headlong down a path that would lead to war.

might seem weak, but when would they be stronger? The colonists were defending their own country. They had a strong desire for liberty, they were brave, and their cause was just. Think seriously, he said in his Liberty or Death speech, about the English responses to our earlier requests. Sending troops to close Boston Harbor was hardly a sign of peaceful intentions.

Patrick Henry declared that the arrival of the British navy and army could mean only one thing. England was preparing to force the colonies to submit to the will of the king and Parliament. Forced submission to the British crown and Parliament would place the colonies at the mercy of the king. Their freedom and self-government would be lost forever. Look to the north, he said. If the British conquered Boston and New York, they would do the same in Virginia unless the colony prepared for war.

"It is in vain, sir, to extenuate the matter. Gentleman may cry, peace, peace—but there is no peace. The war is actually begun. The next gale that sweeps from the North will bring to our ears the clash of resounding arms!"

Patrick Henry reached into his pocket and clasped his hand around an ivory letter opener.

"Our brethren are already in the field! Why stand we here idle? What is it that gentlemen wish? What would they have? Is life so dear or peace so sweet, as to be purchased at the price of chains and slavery?"

He raised the letter opener as though it were a

dagger aimed at his heart.

"Forbid it Almighty God! I know not what course others may take; but as for me, give me liberty or give me death!"

For effect, Henry suddenly made the motion of plunging the weapon toward his chest.

It was time to vote. Patrick Henry had delivered one of the most dramatic and important speeches in history. It changed men's minds and gave them courage. Patrick Henry's resolution to prepare an army for defense of the Virginia colony passed 65 to 60. Virginia would make ready to defend herself against British attack.

8. "Gale from the North"

A few short weeks after Patrick Henry had predicted dire news from the North, messengers brought word of the battle. On April 19, 1775, the Revolutionary War began between the British army and the Massachusetts militiamen at Lexington and Concord. That same month, in the middle of the night, Governor Dunmore of Virginia sent the royal marines to remove the public gunpowder from the magazine in Williamsburg to keep the patriots from using it against the British. Patrick Henry himself gathered a group of 150 Hanover County men to march on Williamsburg and demand the return of the public gunpowder. Governor Dunmore denounced "Patrick Henry and his deluded followers." A few weeks later, on June 8, 1775, Dunmore and his family slipped out of their palace in Williamsburg and took refuge

John Murray Dunmore was born in 1732, in Britain. He became royal governor of Virginia in 1771, until he was kicked out of America in 1775.

This engraving showing the Battle of Lexington, which was fought on April 19, 1775, was created by a French artist named F. Godfrey. The battle marked the beginning of the Revolutionary War, which the French later would join as American allies.

aboard a British warship anchored in the York River.

The collapse of royal government brought confusion to Virginia and the other colonies. For years, people had focused on wrongs that needed to be corrected. Now they had to figure out how best to start over. "I have but one lamp by which my feet are guided," Henry had told the delegates at St. John's Church, "and that is the lamp of experience. I know of no way of judging the future but by the past." Even people who agree to learn from history, however, can disagree about the exact lessons it teaches.

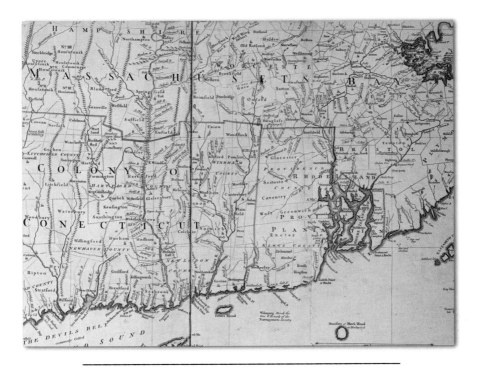

This 1774 map by Jeffreys shows the most inhabited part of New England, including Massachusetts. Massachusetts was the site of much of the action at the beginning of the war. The Boston Tea Party occurred in Boston Harbor in 1773. Then in 1775, the Battles of Lexington and Concord occurred, starting the Revolutionary War.

History offered very few examples of successful republics. Ancient Greece and early Rome were the patriots' favorite models, but history gave them much to worry about. Revolutions usually brought civil war. They often ended in anarchy or tyranny.

A month after Dunmore had evacuated the Governor's Palace, delegates to Virginia's Third Convention met in Richmond. Their task was to create a new government, but they found themselves "of as many different opinions as we are men—undoing one day, what we did the day

Patrick Henry's resignation as commander in chief was not without bitterness. At the head of the Committee of Safety was Edmund Pendleton, who often disagreed with Patrick Henry in the Conventions. Henry felt insulted that the committee appointed Colonel Woodford, a younger but more experienced officer, to command the expedition against Lord Dunmore. Opportunity for military achievement was rare in Virginia and Henry felt the task should have been his. It seemed the committee was purposely refusing him any opportunity of an engagement. When he resigned in March 1776, many claimed that the Committee had forced him to resign.

before." They argued about many things, but especially the militia and its officers.

Patrick Henry had no military experience except for leading the Hanover militia toward Williamsburg to rescue the colony's gunpowder. Nevertheless, he was chosen to be colonel and commander in chief of the Virginia Militia. It was not a wise choice. "I think my countrymen made a capital mistake," General George Washington said, "when they took Henry out of the senate to place him in the field." Washington knew that his friend could do more good for America as a legislator than as a commander. "Pity it is," he concluded, "that [Henry] does not see this, and remove [himself] by a voluntary resignation." Henry lacked the experience to train his men well, and had to rely on advisers when making military decisions.

In the autumn of 1775, Dunmore sent British troops to attack Norfolk and Portsmouth, centers of trade and shipbuilding in Virginia. The patriot forces needed skilled and experienced leadership. Faced with a military emergency, the Committee of Safety assigned Henry only the task of defending Williamsburg. They sent a more experienced officer, William Woodford, to command the counterattack against Lord Dunmore.

Much to the disappointment of his troops, Patrick Henry resigned from his position as commander early in 1776. His men loved him and enjoyed serving under him, but when some of them talked of resigning from the militia, Patrick Henry and other leaders convinced them to accept the leadership of Colonel Woodford. Although "prevented from serving his country in a military capacity," Henry proclaimed, his talents "would ever be exerted in support of the glorious cause." As Washington said, Henry's talents were more valuable in government than on the field of battle.

On the following spread: This is a 1775 map of Virginia. Note that Norfolk has been highlighted on the map. Portsmouth would have been nearby. Both towns were centers for trade and shipbuilding and therefore primary targets for the British. Although Patrick Henry was commander in chief of the militia, he was inexperienced. It was important that the colonists did not lose control of the seaports, therefore they sent a more experienced officer to defend Norfolk and Portsmouth.

CAROLINA

Trade, Soil and Produce of VIRGINIA.

...generally a black deep Soil and produces the largest Tobacco, and all other Plants, and as the Country abounds in large Navigable Rivers ...
...eat proportion of the Land is of this kind the produce of which is very easily brought to Market, but the Land that lies distant from the ...
...rs is generally of a middling Quality yet produces Maize or Indian Corn sufficient for the supply of the Inhabitants who chiefly use Bread ...
...de from this Grain and the very meanest and hilly Lands are very proper for the Peach Tree, every Planter having an Orchard of those ...
...the Brandy made from that Fruit being excellent, and indeed might be made in sufficient Quantities for the supply of the People, was ...

9. Governor Henry

On April 19, 1776, exactly one year after "the shot heard 'round the world," the voters of Hanover County elected Patrick Henry and his stepbrother John Syme to represent them in Virginia's Fifth Revolutionary Convention.

The convention worked hard in May and June 1776. It declared Virginia independent of Great Britain and adopted its first state constitution. The Constitution included the Virginia Declaration of Rights, an important forerunner of the Bill of Rights. Henry's lifelong ally, George Mason, was the main author of the state Constitution and first fourteen clauses of the Declaration of Rights. Patrick Henry added a guarantee of religious toleration and the reminder "that no free government . . . can be preserved to any people but by a firm adherence to justice, moderation, temperance, frugality, and virtue, and by frequent recurrence to fundamental principles."

June 29, 1776, was a great day for Virginia. On that Saturday, the convention formally adopted the Constitution and chose Patrick Henry as the first governor of the independent commonwealth, or republic, of

Ralph Waldo Emerson

The "shot heard 'round the world" refers to the first battle of the Revolution, at Concord, Massachusetts, April 19, 1775. The phrase comes from the "Concord Hymn," a poem written by Ralph Waldo Emerson and read at the completion of the Concord Monument, July 4, 1837.

"The Concord Hymn"

By the rude bridge that arched the flood,
Their flag to April's breeze unfurled,
Here once the embattled farmers stood,
And fired the shot heard 'round the world.
The foe long since in silence slept;
Alike the conqueror silent sleeps;
And Time the ruined bridge has swept
Down the dark stream which seaward creeps.
On this green bank, by this soft stream,
We set to-day a votive stone;
That memory may their deed redeem,
When, like our sires, our sons are gone.
Spirit, that made those heroes dare
To die, or leave their children free,
Bid Time and Nature gently spare
The shaft we raise to them and thee.

Virginia's first state constitution and declaration of rights were approved in June 1776. The Declaration of Rights was an important forerunner to the Bill of Rights in the American Constitution. The purpose of the Declaration of Rights was to secure the rights of the people before giving the government any power.

Virginia. He served three one-year terms as governor of Virginia, the largest of the American states. Despite the severely limited powers allowed to the early Virginia governors, Patrick Henry did everything he could to help win the war for independence and liberty.

As the first elected governor of the newly independent state, Patrick Henry had many things to do. However, the first letter he wrote as governor of Virginia was not to a politician or military officer. Governor Henry addressed his very first letter to the ministers of the Baptist

Churches in Virginia. Under the royal government, Baptist preachers often had been arrested and jailed for disturbing the peace. Henry had supported religious dissenters in the past. Now as governor, he hoped that all denominations—whether Baptists, Presbyterians, Episcopalians, or Quakers—could put aside their differences and join together as brothers in faith. "My constant Endeavor shall be to guard the Rights of all my Fellow-citizens from every Encroachment," he wrote.

> *"I am happy to find a [universal] spirit prevailing in our country, and that those religious Distinctions, which formerly produced some heats, are now forgotten. . . . My most earnest Wish is, that Christian Charity, Forbearance and Love may unite all our different Persuasions as Brethren who must perish or triumph together; and I trust that the Time is not far distant when we shall greet each other as peaceable Possessors of that just and equal System of Liberty adopted by the last Convention, and in Support of which may God crown our Arms with Success."*

Patrick Henry also kept his word to the militiamen he had commanded in 1775. During his first years as governor, Patrick Henry worked with the governors of Maryland and North Carolina to unite their forces against the British. Across the Appalachian Mountains, where Virginia claimed

This map of Virginia was created by Fry and Jefferson in 1775. This map shows the territory around the Ohio River and the Appalachian Mountains that Patrick Henry worked so hard to protect.

territory along the Ohio and Mississippi Rivers, he worked to protect frontiersmen from attack by the British and their Native American allies. Patrick Henry directed Virginia troops in the west to protect any person who showed that he or she was an American citizen.

Governor Henry also worked with the Virginia delegates in Congress and with General George Washington to support the American army fighting against the British. In his letters to the Congress, Patrick Henry urged that the troops be vaccinated against smallpox, which was sweeping across the country and killing many people. He wanted to make sure the troops did not spread the disease, and he politely demanded that Congress pay for the vaccine:

> *"The Troops will I doubt not be under a necessity of Inoculation for the Small pox. This will delay their progress and occasion expense. As the battalion is ordered into the Continental Service, it is not doubted but that the Continent will defray every expense necessarily incurred thereby."*

Patrick Henry respected Washington's military experience. He sought his friend's advice whenever important military decisions had to be made. In September 1777, Henry reminded General George Washington that "in every military measure" the governor of Virginia would "be solely guided by your opinions." Governor Henry also supported Washington and the American troops in any way he could. During the grim winter of 1777–1778, Washington's army camped at Valley Forge, Pennsylvania, without adequate food, fuel, or supplies. In Virginia, Patrick Henry was busy collecting blankets, woolen clothes, boots, and food for the Continental army. Henry gathered supplies from every corner of Virginia.

The winter at Valley Forge was a harsh one for the American troops. Men were starving and freezing to death. Many soldiers chose to desert the army during this winter. Washington was proud of the men who chose to remain. He believed their willingness to deal with such hard times for the American cause spoke volumes about the righteousness of their fight for independence from Britain.

He sent agents to other states to buy supplies from their merchants. He seized supplies from enemy ships and wagons. He negotiated with the Spanish governors of Cuba and Louisiana to provide the patriot forces with supplies and money. In addition to blankets and food, Patrick Henry sent ten tons of lead to the Virginia troops so they could make bullets. He also sent sulfur and other materials for them to make gunpowder. Although the governor's official powers were severely limited by the Constitution of Virginia, Patrick Henry used his influence and authority to ensure that Virginia troops had the supplies they needed.

Governor Patrick Henry pleaded with the Spanish governors of Louisiana and Cuba for their help. He knew a relationship with them could be invaluable to the war effort and Virginia in general.

Indeed, Governor Henry showed great foresight. He promoted trade between the American states and the Spanish colonies of Louisiana and Cuba long before Thomas Jefferson bought the Louisiana territory in 1803. Henry told the governor of Cuba:

This map shows the route that was followed down the Mississippi between Virginia and New Orleans.

"We could by an easy inland Navigation, bring [goods] down the Mississippi to New Orleans from our back Country, in exchange for your Woolens, Linens, Wines, [and] Military Stores."

To the governor at New Orleans he offered "Immense Quantities of Hemp, Flax, Skins, Furs, Beef, Pork, Flour, Staves, [and] Shingles." His vision was international in scope:

"the produce of our back Country might be easily carried down the Mississippi to New Orleans, which place, if it were made a free Port, would be resorted to by the French & Dutch who might take off the Tobacco & other Articles which Spain would not want for her own Consumption."

His letters and diplomacy worked. The governor of Louisiana sent supplies and money up the Mississippi River, and Henry secretly sent a military force to get it.

Patrick Henry dispatched Colonel George Rogers Clark on the secret mission down the Ohio River to the point where it joins the Mississippi River. The mission was such an important secret that Governor Henry could not even mention the specific names of places in his letters to Clark. Colonel Clark had orders to build a fort at the mouth of the Ohio River so the British could not attack from the west. In the colonial past, frontier warfare often had seen atrocities committed by rival

George Rogers Clark was born in 1752 in Caroline, Virginia. In 1772, he and some other men settled in Kentucky. When war broke out, Clark went to see Patrick Henry. Virginia granted Kentucky 500 pounds of gunpowder for their defense, and made them a county of Virginia.

European troops or their Native American allies. Governor Henry instructed Clark to respect American citizens and treat British prisoners decently.

"It is earnestly desired that you show Humanity to such British Subjects and other persons as fall in your hands. . . . Assistance and protection against all Enemies whatever shall be afforded them & the Commonwealth of Virginia is pledged to accomplish it. But if these people will not accede to these reasonable Demands, they must feel the miseries of War, under the direction of that Humanity that has hitherto distinguished Americans, & which it is expected you will ever consider as the Rule of your Conduct & from which you are in no Instance to depart."

Once the supplies and money from Louisiana arrived at the new fort, Clark was to escort them safely back to Virginia so the supplies could be sent to the troops fighting the British.

Despite Governor Henry's overwhelming desire to see American troops defeat the British and their Native American allies on the western frontier, Henry gave his officers orders to treat women and children with respect and to punish the enemy men appropriately, but not savagely. The welfare of all the Virginian troops was a concern, but the Culpeper County militia (sometimes spelled Culpepper) may have enjoyed the governor's favor. The Culpeper militia wore hunting shirts with the slogan from Patrick Henry's famous speech, Liberty or Death. The county had sent so many volunteers that Henry worried that Culpeper County could lose all its men to the war. In a letter dated July 27, 1777, Henry told General Edward Hand: "Culpeper County has furnished so many men I Should be glad you'd Spare them if possible."

This is the flag of the Culpeper militia. The flag had Patrick Henry's words on it as well as a picture of a rattlesnake saying "Don't tread on me." This was a warning to the British that the colonies would fight back. It also symbolized that the American colonists were like a rattlesnake—they would strike only if they were in danger or provoked. The thirteen rattles meant that the thirteen colonies, protests would be heard only if they were united.

10. Friends to Fight with Us

The war for independence began in New England, and at first the British army attempted to defeat the Americans in the North. They captured New York City, at the mouth of the Hudson River. Then they sent another army south from Montreal, Canada, to cut off New England from the other states. Patrick Henry, in his Liberty or Death speech, had expressed confidence that "three millions of people, armed in the holy cause of liberty . . . are invincible by any force which our enemy can send against us." After two years, however, Washington's army did not feel invincible. At best, they had won a few skirmishes and avoided capture.

In public debate and in private conversations, Henry always counted on help from Spain and especially from France. "We shall not fight our battles alone," he had said at St. John's Church. "There is a just God who presides over the destinies of nations, and who will raise up friends to fight our battles for us." France, however, was reluctant to join the Americans until they demonstrated a good chance of winning the war.

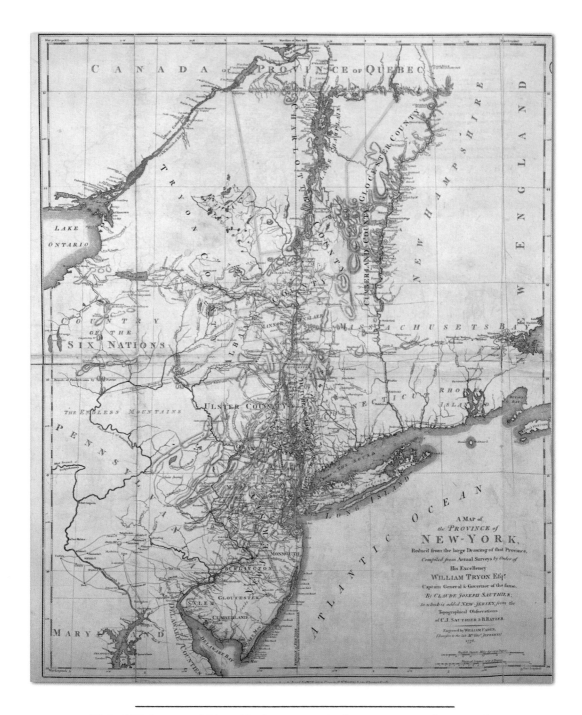

This 1776 map of New York was made from surveys done at the time. It combines information from a map by William Tryon, Claude Joseph Sauthier, and B. Razer. William Faden created this engraving.

This engraving by an unknown artist shows the surrender of General Burgoyne at Saratoga on October 17, 1777. This battle was a turning point in the war, as it convinced the French to join the battle against the British. The French provided much-needed supplies and men.

On October 17, 1777, as 9,000 British soldiers marched south toward New York City from Montreal, they were trapped at Saratoga, New York. The British general, John Burgoyne, surrendered his entire army. Here was proof, as Henry had promised, that "the battle . . . is not to the strong alone," but "to the vigilant, the active, the brave." Burgoyne's surrender changed history. France entered the war against Great Britain.

On October 31, Governor Henry proclaimed a day of thanksgiving:

Whereas I have received certain intelligence, that General Gates, after repeated advantages gained over General Burgoyne, compelled him on the 14th day of this month to surrender himself and his whole army. . . . to the end that we may not, through a vain and presumptuous confidence in our own strength, be led away to forget the hand of Heaven, whose assistance we . . . have experienced in the signal success of the arms of the United States . . . I have thought proper, by and with the advice of the Council of State, to appoint Thursday — the thirteenth day of the next month to be observed, in all churches and congregations of Christians throughout this State, as a day of general and solemn thanksgiving; and it is most earnestly recommended to the several Ministers and teachers of the Gospel, . . . to embrace this opportunity of impressing on the minds of their hearers those sentiments of pious joy which the glorious occasion so aptly calls for.

Given under my hand at the Council Chamber, in the city of Williamsburg, the 31st day of October, in the second year of the Commonwealth, Annoque Domini 1777.

P. HENRY
GOD save the UNITED STATES.

11. War and Peace

While Governor Henry was busy looking out for Virginia and the American troops, he was also busy with his family. In 1777, about one year after he was elected for his first term as the first governor of independent Virginia, Patrick Henry married Dorothea Dandridge. Her grandfather, Alexander Spotswood, had been governor of Virginia in the 1720s. She and Patrick had their first child in August 1778. Dorothea, named after her mother, was the only child of a nonroyal Virginia governor born in the Governor's Palace at Williamsburg. A year later, after finishing his third term as governor, Patrick moved his family to Leatherwood, a 10,000-acre plantation near the Virginia-North Carolina border. The voters of Henry County, named in his honor in 1776, promptly elected him to the General Assembly.

Dorothea Dandridge was born in 1755 and died at Seven Islands, near Red Hill, in 1831.

After General Burgoyne's surrender in New York, the war moved south. The British captured Charleston, South Carolina, in 1780. From there, General Charles Cornwallis marched north toward Virginia.

Thomas Jefferson, author of the Declaration of Independence, was elected governor of Virginia after Patrick Henry. Near the end of his term of office, the

This oil painting of Thomas Jefferson was made by Gilbert Stuart, a well-known artist who lived from 1755 to 1828. Thomas Jefferson was born on April 13, 1743, and would die on July 14, 1826. Jefferson would become the third president of the United States in 1800.

British cavalry led by Benedict Arnold and Banistre Tarleton raided Richmond, Charlottesville, and Monticello. To escape capture, Jefferson and the legislature, including Henry, fled over the Blue Ridge Mountains to Staunton. Later the American army and French navy ended the war by forcing Cornwallis to surrender at Yorktown in October 1781.

A man who did not like Jefferson asked the legislature to investigate his conduct as governor. Patrick Henry, who knew that the facts would show Governor Jefferson had acted properly, supported the investigation.

This color engraving of the Battle of Yorktown was created in the 1780s by an artist named Mondhare. At the Battle of Yorktown in Pennsylvania in 1781, British General Cornwallis lost the decisive battle that ended the American Revolution. The ships at the right were French Admiral DeGrasse's fleet that helped seal Cornwallis's fate.

The legislature of Virginia declared its "high opinion of Mr. Jefferson's ability, rectitude, and integrity, as Chief Magistrate of this Commonwealth." Unfortunately, Governor Jefferson regarded the investigation as a personal insult and blamed Henry for it. Their friendship turned sour. Thomas Jefferson never thought kindly of Patrick Henry again.

12. Virtue or Wickedness?

In the spring of 1783, George Mason congratulated Patrick Henry on their accomplishments. Twenty eventful years had passed since Henry's speech at Hanover Courthouse on The Parsons' Cause. He had been accused of treason against the king. Now he was respected as a founder of the republic. America had won a place "among the nations of the world," Mason proudly wrote.

Mason and Henry had worked together against the Stamp Act and for independence and the Virginia Declaration of Rights. Now the war for independence was over. America's revolutionary experiment, an elected government dedicated to liberty, had just begun. Now George Mason asked Henry a big question: "Whether our Independence shall prove a blessing or a curse?" The answer, they both knew, "must depend on our own wisdom or folly, virtue or wickedness."

Patrick Henry was 47 years old. Washington was 51. Mason was 58. Jefferson was 40. They were no longer young patriots attacking a distant king. In the twenty

George Mason lived from 1725 to 1792. Mason wrote the Declaration of Rights and most of the Virginia Constitution. He refused to sign the American Constitution because it gave kinglike powers to the central government. Pressure from men such as Mason and Henry ensured that a Bill of Rights, protecting individual rights, was added.

years since The Parsons' Cause, they had become sea-
soned statesmen. Now their task was to build a free
and independent nation for the next generation.

At Leatherwood, the Henry family continued to
grow. Sarah Butler was born there in 1780, Martha
Catharina in 1781, and Patrick Jr. in 1783. Their father
was busy with his law practice, and again busy in the
legislature of Virginia.

Patrick Henry owned slaves. His plantations, like
others throughout Virginia and the South, depended on
their labor. Like many slave owners during the
Revolution, however, he hated slavery. "In a country,
above all others, fond of liberty," he wrote, slavery was
"repugnant to humanity, . . . inconsistent with the
Bible, and destructive to morality."

Henry knew that slavery was "totally repugnant
to the first impressions of right and wrong." He
admired the Baptists and Quakers who gave freedom to
their slaves. "Henry was," Jefferson remembered, "even
more determined in his opposition to slavery than the
rest of us." Virginia did not end slavery, but "through
the influence of Patrick Henry," Jefferson said, Virginia
found "the moral courage to take a bold and decided
stand." Laws were passed to end the slave trade from
Africa into Virginia. The state of Virginia also made it
easier for slave owners to free their slaves. "Would anyone believe I am the master of slaves of my own purchase?" Henry wrote. "I am drawn along by the general

inconvenience of living here without them. I will not, I cannot justify it."

On his plantations, slaves were taught to read the Bible. Some learned trades such as tanning leather, carpentry, blacksmithing, or distilling whiskey from corn. Most of Henry's slaves—he owned more than ninety when he died—raised his tobacco and corn, horses, pigs, and cows. Henry believed that "a time will come . . . to abolish this lamentable evil." Until then, he said, "let us transmit to our descendants, together with our slaves, . . . an abhorrence of slavery. . . . Let us treat the unhappy victims with lenity. It is the furthest advance we can make toward justice. . . . The purity of our religion . . . is at variance with that law which warrants slavery."

Freedom of religion was another important value for Patrick Henry. In the 1760s, he had attacked the Anglican clergy as "enemies of the community." In the 1770s he had defended Baptist preachers jailed for disturbing the peace. In Hanover and later in Prince Edward and Charlotte Counties, his neighbors and friends included Presbyterians, Quakers, and Methodists as well as Episcopalians (as Anglicans became known after the Revolution). Henry remained a member of the Episcopal church, but in 1783 he helped the Presbyterians pass a law creating Hampden-Sydney College in Prince Edward County. Six of his sons studied there. Wisdom and virtue were essential

Patrick Henry felt that people needed religious as well as academic instruction, and that government was responsible for providing it. He helped form Hampden Sydney-College because of this belief.

guardians of freedom. Henry believed that "every free state" should promote "useful knowledge amongst its citizens."

A year later, Henry wrote a law to support teachers of the Christian religion. In addition to their Sunday preaching, Virginia's Episcopalian and Presbyterian ministers often taught school during the week. Henry proposed to expand government support of these teachers. Many Baptists, Methodists, and Quakers opposed his idea. They had long suffered persecution by the state-supported church and did not want its power to increase.

This map was created in 1783. Notice the pink state at the right. This is Virginia as it was in 1783. All the land in the upper left that is colored green shows the land that Virginia gave to the new nation when independence was achieved.

Henry's bill was defeated in 1784, after he left the legislature to serve two more terms as governor. In its place, Virginia passed Jefferson's Statute for Religious Freedom, which created the principle of separation of church and state. Jefferson also linked a statewide educational system to his declaration of religious liberty, but it took him forty years to pass the law creating the University of Virginia.

Governor once more, Patrick Henry was again responsible for the defense of Virginia. When the war ended, the

Continental army sent its men home. Each state had its own militia, and Governor Henry spent much time organizing the troops in all Virginia's counties.

From its earliest settlement, Virginia claimed land as far west as the Mississippi River and as far north as the modern state of Wisconsin. Other states were jealous of Virginia's western lands, especially states like Maryland and Connecticut, which had no open land to the west. George Rogers Clark and other Virginia soldiers had been promised land for serving in the Revolution. Patrick Henry insisted that part of the Ohio Valley be given to them. Then Virginia gave the rest of the Old Northwest—the modern states of Ohio, Indiana, Illinois, Michigan, and Wisconsin—to the new nation.

Other rivalries between the thirteen states were more lasting. Thousands of Americans were moving across the Appalachian Mountains into the Ohio Valley. In 1785, the first riverboat from Kentucky floated its cargo downstream to Spanish New Orleans, near the mouth of the Mississippi River. At the same time, a New York diplomat, the future chief justice John Jay, was negotiating a treaty with Spain. John Jay suggested that, in exchange for trade and fishing rights that would help New England, America might agree not to use the Mississippi River for 25 years! Patrick Henry and the Virginians were outraged. How would western farmers ship their flour, beef, corn, hogs, and lumber to market if they could not use the Ohio and Mississippi Rivers? John Jay's pro-

This portrait of John Jay was painted by John Trumbull, who painted many politicians from 1804 to 1808. John Jay lived from 1745 to 1829. Along with Alexander Hamilton and James Madison, John Jay wrote and anonymously published *The Federalist*, a series of essays in defense of the Constitution of 1787. Jay wrote five of the essays, warning that rejection of the federal form of government would worsen the rifts forming among the thirteen states.

posal was defeated in Congress, but it made Patrick Henry worry about Virginia's future. He had fought a distant king and parliament when they threatened Virginia. He was not about to allow New York merchants or New England fisherman to hurt his state. Patrick Henry said "he would rather part with the confederation than relinquish the navigation of the Mississippi."

13. We the People?

During Governor Henry's last year in office, 1786, Virginia sent representatives to Annapolis, the capital of Maryland. The conference had been called with the hope of regulating trade between the states. Instead, it became clear that there were larger problems within the Articles of Confederation than a lack of rules for trading between states. So, the Annapolis conference suggested that all thirteen states send delegates to Philadelphia in the summer of 1787. Virginia sent seven fine men to Philadelphia, with instructions to make changes in the Articles of Confederation, which joined the states in a loose union.

Patrick Henry chose not to go. His health was starting to be a problem, but he had other reasons for staying home. His children were growing up. He wanted to provide the boys with farms and the girls with dowries to give them a better start in life than he had had. He could not afford the expense of a summer in Philadelphia. Henry also said he smelt a rat! When John Jay proposed closing the Mississippi River, Patrick

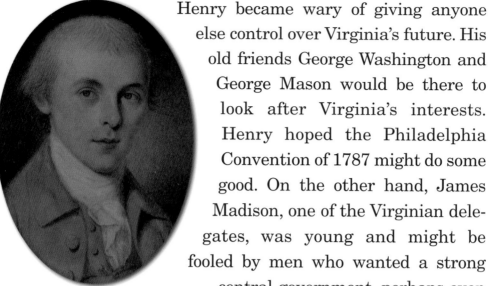

This is a portrait of James Madison (1751–1836) as a young man.

Henry became wary of giving anyone else control over Virginia's future. His old friends George Washington and George Mason would be there to look after Virginia's interests. Henry hoped the Philadelphia Convention of 1787 might do some good. On the other hand, James Madison, one of the Virginian delegates, was young and might be fooled by men who wanted a strong central government, perhaps even a king. Patrick Henry would have to wait and see what came out of the Philadelphia Convention.

The Philadelphia Convention met in secret for months. On September 17, it published a new plan of government. The new Constitution, which now has been in force for more than 200 years, shocked Patrick Henry. It proposed a strong central government. The president had powers that looked like a king's. The federal courts threatened the powers of the states and counties. The new government would have authority to levy taxes, regulate trade, declare war, and make treaties. Worst of all, the convention had rejected George Mason's demand for a bill of rights. Mason refused to sign the Constitution.

All the liberties they had fought for seemed, once again, at risk. Patrick Henry and George Mason were

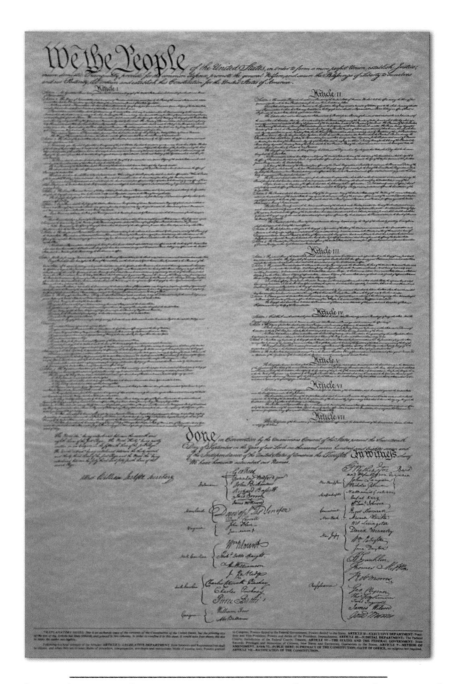

This is the original U.S. Constitution created in 1787 and approved by the states in 1788. This document and its Bill of Rights have become a model for democratic governments around the world.

partners again, this time working to defeat or at least amend the Constitution of 1787. Through the winter of 1787–1788, Americans argued over the proposed Constitution. Its supporters called themselves Federalists. Henry was an anti-Federalist. Many Virginians were undecided. Voters in each county chose two men to meet in Richmond and decide whether to ratify, or approve, the new plan of government. Virginia was the oldest, largest, wealthiest, and most influential state of all. The convention that met in Richmond on June 2, 1788, would decide the fate of the Constitution and the young nation. The outcome was too close to call. About 80 delegates were ready to vote for the Constitution as it was. Another 80 men were ready to vote against it unless drastic changes were made. About two dozen delegates were undecided. The Federalist leaders, James Madison, John Marshall, and Henry Lee, knew that anything could happen. Their opponents included George Mason, Benjamin Harrison, James Monroe, and a man who was already famous as one of history's greatest orators, Patrick Henry.

This is an engraving of anti-Federalist James Monroe, who lived from 1758 to 1831.

In one important detail, this convention was different from

all other occasions on which Henry spoke. Tape recorders and video cameras were not yet invented, but a young man named William Robertson had come to the debates prepared to write down everything that anyone said. Because Robertson captured most of Patrick Henry's words in shorthand with pen and ink, students of American government have been studying his speeches for 200 years.

Day after day, Patrick Henry attacked specific parts of the Constitution. "The first thing I have at heart is American liberty," he said. "The second thing is American union." A powerful central government, far removed from the citizens of Virginia, "will plunge us into misery, and our republic will be lost." He denounced the Constitution as a consolidated government that would destroy the proper authority of the states. "What right had they to say, We the People?. . . instead of We the States?" The Constitution was "pernicious, impolitic, and dangerous." It represented "a revolution as radical as that which separated us from Great Britain." Patrick Henry demanded a bill of rights to protect individual liberties. He also wanted twenty major amendments to protect the authority of state and local governments. Most of all, he wanted to limit the central government's power of taxation.

Patrick Henry's Federalist opponents feared that he was trying to divide "the Union into several Confederacies." Henry replied that "the example of

Virginia is a powerful thing." If there was any chance of amending the Constitution, "her example will have powerful influence—her rejections [of the Constitution] will procure amendments." When the final vote was taken, Virginia ratified the Constitution by a vote of 89 to 79. Henry's strong arguments, however, led to the adoption of 10 amendments to the Constitution, our federal Bill of Rights, in December 1791.

14. The Blessings of Liberty

A few days after Virginia approved the new Constitution, the legislature met in the newly completed Capitol on Shockoe Hill in Richmond. Patrick Henry and his friends once again dominated the state legislature. James Madison, author of the Constitution, hoped that Virginia would send him to the U. S. Senate. He was defeated through Patrick Henry's influence, and Virginia elected anti-Federalists Richard Henry Lee and Theodorick Bland as its first senators. It was a clear message for Madison to follow through on his promise to steer a bill of rights through Congress. The federal bill of rights, adopted in 1791, owes its existence to Patrick Henry, George Mason, and their anti-Federalist allies.

At the end of 1791, Patrick Henry withdrew from politics. "I

Anti-Federalist Richard Henry Lee lived from 1732 to 1794. He was a signer of the Declaration of Independence.

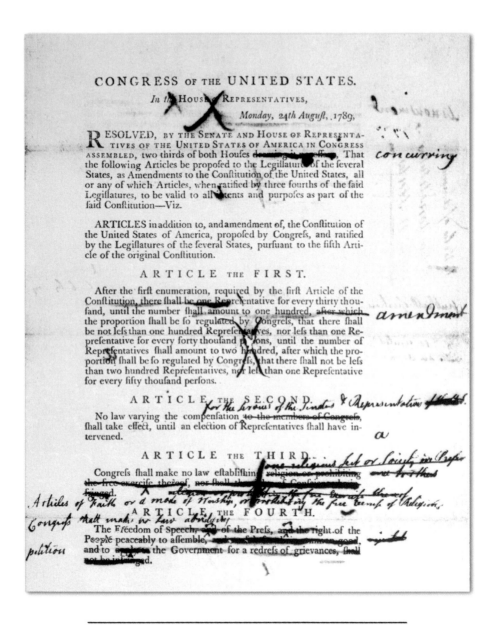

This is a copy of the the first page of the Bill of Rights as it was passed to the House of Representatives in 1789. Notice all the handwritten changes that were marked on the draft. The men who created the Bill of Rights worked very hard to make sure the document would protect the individual rights of the people.

am obliged to be very industrious . . . to clear myself of Debt," he told his children. "I hope to be able to accomplish this in a year or two, if it pleases God to continue me in health and strength."

Henry's legal skills and reputation in the courtroom were in great demand. Through his legal practice, he became one of the hundred wealthiest men in Virginia. His landholdings included three plantations in the foothills of the Blue Ridge Mountains along the Staunton River as it flows east toward Albemarle Sound in North Carolina. After 25 years in Virginia's legislature, five conventions, and five exhausting terms as governor, Patrick and Dorothea Henry retired with their family to the rolling farmland of south central Virginia.

Of the three plantations, his daughters preferred the social life at Red Hill. Their father did not object. He loved nature, and called Red Hill "one of the garden spots of the world." Despite his wealth, Henry chose to live modestly in a small and crowded house. In the main room of the house, on festive occasions, Patrick played his violin and Dorothea played the lute, a stringed instrument like a guitar. On the east end of the house, he and Dorothea added a bedroom for themselves, where they could "hear the patter of rain on its roof." The youngest children had a nursery at the west end of the house. The older daughters shared two small rooms upstairs. Their older brothers, along with young men

Red Hill was the final home of patriot and statesman Patrick Henry. He lived here from 1793 to 1799, and is buried here with his wife Dorothea. Red Hill is located in Brookneal, Virginia.

who studied law with the great patriot, slept in a room in the law office, about 70 yards (.06 km) north of the house.

With his large family, 90 slaves, young law students, and a constant stream of visitors and friends, the 2,090-acre (845.8-ha) plantation at Red Hill was like a village. Henry rose early. "In the mornings of the spring, summer, and fall, while the air was cool and calm," the great orator climbed a watchtower on the crest of the hill and "gave orders and directions to his servants at work a half-mile distant from him" in the valley below. Near the tower stood several cabins for his slaves. The rest lived in cabins along a ridge to the west called the Quarter Place. On the hillside to the east, Henry's slaves operated his tannery, distillery, blacksmith shop, and laundry.

Things were less peaceful in the world beyond the hills of Campbell and Charlotte Counties. The French Revolution had begun in 1789, with promises of "Liberty, Equality, and Fraternity." It quickly turned vicious and bloody. King Louis XVI, a succession of revolutionary leaders, and thousands of ordinary people

Red Hill, Patrick Henry's final home, was a huge plantation. It was more like a small village than a home. It had a blacksmith shop, illustrated above, where items such as horseshoes were made from iron. It also had a tannery, where animal hides were tanned to make clothing.

died on the guillotine in Paris and in other cities. Thousands more escaped into exile. That same year, Americans inaugurated George Washington as their first president. Patrick Henry's old friend soon saw his administration split between his secretary of the treasury, Alexander Hamilton, and his secretary of state, Thomas Jefferson. Hamilton's fellow New Yorker, John Jay, negotiated another treaty that favored New England and hurt the south. To make things worse, war broke out between Great Britain, still a constitutional monarchy, and the revolutionary French republic. The Federalists, who were strong in New England, worried that America might follow the example of France. In 1798, they passed laws called the Alien and Sedition Acts and used them to imprison newspaper editors or politicians who criticized their officials. In response, the legislatures of Kentucky and Virginia passed resolutions, written by James Madison and Thomas Jefferson. They declared the Alien and Sedition Acts unconstitutional, and reminded the Federalists that their states could pull out of the union.

From his retirement, Henry watched these developments with alarm. He saw President Washington "most abusively treated." The rising greatness of America, he felt, was "greatly tarnished by the general prevalence of deism, which . . . is but another name for vice and depravity." Worst of all, these were all things he had predicted in the convention of 1788. He was especially

This oil painting of George Washington was created from life by Gilbert Stuart in 1796. The unfinished painting was used as a study for a full-length portrait that had been commissioned as a gift for the Earl of Shelburne. He used the likeness in many subsequent portraits he did of Washington because of the demand there was for his likeness.

disappointed in Madison and Jefferson. "What must I think of those men whom I myself warned of the danger," he asked in a letter to his daughter. "The policy of these men, both then and now, appears to me quite void of wisdom and foresight."

Dwindling health and the needs of his family prompted Henry to decline appointments to high office. He said no when Governor Henry Lee wanted him to represent Virginia in the U. S. Senate. He said no when President Washington wanted to appoint him Chief Justice of the Supreme Court, Secretary of State, or minister to Spain or France. He even turned down a sixth term as governor of Virginia.

This is an engraving of Henry Lee, governor of Virginia from 1792 to 1795. As a scout during the war, he earned the nickname Lighthorse Harry for making lightning raids against the enemy.

Only a direct appeal from George Washington persuaded Henry to stand for election to the Virginia legislature in 1799. Partisan strife, echoing the bloody scenes of the French Revolution, threatened to undermine the young republic. The repressive Alien and Sedition Acts prompted opponents to assert that states could nullify acts of the federal government. "At such a crisis as this," Washington wrote in a private letter to Henry, "measures are systematically . . . pursued which must eventually dissolve the union or produce coercion." Washington expressed his "earnest wish that you will come forward for the ensuing elections for Congress or the state legislature." He told Henry, "Your weight of character and influence would be a bulwark against . . . dangerous sentiments" and "a rallying point for the timid."

Bowed with age, his health precarious, Patrick Henry made his last public oration to the voters at Charlotte County Courthouse in March 1799. He appealed for unity and moderation. "Let us not split into factions which must destroy that union upon

The Charlotte County Courthouse was the site of Patrick Henry's last public speech. He urged the states to work together and remember the reasons they had fought so hard for independence.

which our existence hangs," he said. If the members of Congress passed bad laws, they should be voted out of office. He reminded his neighbors:

> *"It belonged to the people, who held the reins*
> *over the head of congress, and to them alone, to*
> *say whether they were acceptable or otherwise . . .*
> *If I am asked what is to be done when a people*
> *feel themselves intolerably oppressed, my answer*
> *is ready—overturn the government. But . . . wait*
> *at least until some infringement is made upon*
> *your rights that cannot be otherwise redressed;*
> *for . . . you may bid adieu forever to representa-*
> *tive government. You can never exchange the pre-*
> *sent government but for a monarchy."*

Patrick Henry won the election and returned to Red Hill, never again to leave.

Three months later, on June 6, 1799, Patrick Henry died, "speaking words of love and peace to his family, who were weeping around his chair." He was sixty-three years old. Patrick Henry's tombstone in the cemetery at Red Hill, about 30 yards (27 m) east of his bedroom, bears the inscription, "His fame his best epitaph." Death silenced the patriot known as the Voice of the Revolution, but his words echo into the twenty-first century.

15. "Reader . . .
Remember This"

On June 14, 1799, the *Virginia Gazette* announced the death of Patrick Henry. The editor put a heavy black border around the death notice. "As long as our rivers flow, or mountains stand," said the *Gazette*, "Virginia . . . will say to rising generations, imitate my HENRY." Of all the major leaders of the American Revolution, Patrick Henry was the one person who never held high office outside Virginia. Patrick Henry explained the Revolution to ordinary men and women throughout America in words they understood. They were his neighbors, and he shared their fears and hopes. "It is not now easy to say what we should have done without Patrick Henry," said Thomas Jefferson. "He was before us all in maintaining the spirit of the Revolution."

Near his last will, Patrick Henry left a small envelope sealed with wax. Inside was a single sheet of paper on which he had copied his Resolutions against the Stamp Act. On the back, Patrick Henry left a message that he knew could be read only after his death. It began with a short history of his Resolutions against

Patrick Henry is buried at Red Hill, his final home and
the place where he enjoyed so many peaceful years with
his family. The words on his tombstone are a testimony
to the greatness of a patriot whose words still speak to our
hearts more than two centuries after his death.

the Stamp Act. They "spread throughout America with astonishing Quickness." As a result, the colonies united in their "Resistance to British Taxation," and "brought on the War which finally separated the two Countrys and gave Independence to ours."

Whether America's independence "will prove a Blessing or a Curse," Henry continued, "will depend on the Use our people make of the Blessings which a gracious God hath bestowed on us. If they are wise, they will be great and happy. If they are of a contrary Character, they will be miserable. Righteousness alone can exalt them as a Nation.

Reader! whoever thou art, remember this, and in thy Sphere, practice Virtue thyself, and encourage it in others.

P. HENRY"

Timeline

1736	Patrick Henry was born on May 29, 1736.
1751	Henry was apprenticed to a storekeeper.
1752	John Henry set up a store for his sons, William and Patrick. The business failed.
1754–1763	The French and Indian War was fought.
1754	Patrick Henry married Sarah Shelton.
1757	Pine Slash was destroyed by fire. Patrick Henry opened a store, which failed.
1760	Patrick Henry became a lawyer.
1763	The Two-Penny Act was passed, but was overturned by the king of England.
	Patrick Henry argued The Parsons' Cause.
1764	Patrick and Sarah moved to Roundabout.
1765	Patrick Henry was elected to the House of Burgesses in Louisa County.
	On May 29, Henry presented his resolutions against the Stamp Act.
1771	Patrick Henry purchased Scotchtown Plantation.
1772	Robert Carter Nicholas gave his law practice to Patrick Henry.

Henry was a member of the Committee of Correspondence.

1773   Parliament passed the Tea Act. The Boston Tea Party occurred in response.

1774   Patrick Henry was elected as a delegate to the First Continental Congress.

Parliament sent troops to New England and New York.

1775   Sarah died at Scotchtown.

Patrick Henry gave his Liberty or Death speech on March 23.

On April 19, the Battle of Lexington and Concord occurred, beginning the Revolution.

Governor Dunmore of Virginia removed the public gunpowder from Williamsburg.

Patrick Henry and a group of 150 men demanded the return of the gunpowder.

Henry was elected colonel and commander in chief of the Virginia militia.

1776   Henry resigned his military position.

Henry represented Hanover County in Virginia's Fifth Revolutionary Convention.

Virginia adopted its first state constitution.

On June 29, Patrick Henry was elected as the first governor of Virginia. He served three consecutive one-year terms.

1777   Henry married Dorothea Dandridge.

Americans won a major victory at Saratoga.

The French entered the war.

1779   Patrick Henry moved his family to Leatherwood.

Henry was elected to the General Assembly.

1780   The British captured Charleston, SC.

1781   Cornwallis surrendered at Yorktown in October, ending the war.

1784   Statute for Religious Freedom was passed.

Henry served a fourth term as governor.

1785   Henry served a fifth term as governor.

1787   The new Constitution was written and sent to the states for ratification.

1788   Henry was elected to the Virginia House of Delegates and to the Ratifying Convention.

In June, Virginia ratified the Constitution.

1791   Henry retired from the House of Delegates.

1794   Henry purchased Red Hill, in Virginia.

1799   Henry was re-elected to the House of Delegates.

Patrick Henry died at Red Hill on June 6. He outlived six of his seventeen children.

Glossary

adieu (uh-DYOO) French word for farewell or goodbye.

allies (A-lyz) People or nations that agree to help another nation or group of people.

atrocity (uh-TRAH-suh-tee) A wicked, brutal, or cruel act.

benevolence (buh-NEHV-lunts) An act of kindness.

burgess (BUR-juhs) A citizen elected to make laws for colonial Virginia.

cavalry (KA-vuhl-ree) The part of an army that rides horses.

clergy (KLUR-jee) The people with official duties in a church, such as ministers or preachers.

coercion (ko-UR-zhun) The act of forcing a person or thing to do something.

consolidate (kun-SAH-luh-dayt) To join together or unite.

currency (KUHR-ent-see) Paper money or coins in circulation.

deism (DEE-ih-zuhm) A religious point of view that emphasized human reason and morality. In the 1700s, deists rejected the teachings of official churches, doubting a divine Creator could interfere with the universe's natural laws.

depravity (dih-PRA-vuh-tee) The quality or state of being marked by corruption or evil.

dissent (dih-SENT) To differ in opinion. The Christian colonists who did not belong to the Anglican church were called dissenters because they were not members of the Anglican church.

distillery (dih-STIH-luh-ree) A place where whiskey is made.

dowry (DOW-ree) The money or property that a woman brings to her husband when they get married.

eloquence (EH-luh-kwuhnts) The art of powerful and persuasive expression.

epitaph (EH-puh-taf) The words carved in the stone of a tomb or grave in memory of the one buried there, or a brief statement celebrating or remembering a deceased person.

forfeit (FOR-fit) To lose by some error, offense, or crime.

Great Awakening (GRAYT uh-WAY-kuhn-ing) The period of religious activity from 1720 to 1740 in the American colonies. Traveling preachers, like Samuel Davies, excited listeners with sermons meant to "awaken" religious belief.

Homer (HOH-muhr) The great poet of ancient Greece who wrote two long poems, or epics, called *The Iliad* and *The Odyssey*.

industrious (in-DUHS-tree-us) Hardworking or busy.

infringement (in-FRINJ-muhnt) A violation of a right.

jury (JOOR-ee) A group of people chosen to make a decision in a court case based on the facts given to them.

lenity (LEH-nuh-tee) Mildness, leniency.

negotiate (nih-GOH-shee-ayt) To bargain with someone.

nullify (NUH-luh-fy) To counteract completely the force, effectiveness, or value of something.

orator (OR-uh-tuhr) A skillful public speaker.

ordain (or-DAYN) When someone is formally approved for a position of church leadership, such as a priest or a rabbi.

parish (PAR-ish) An area with its own church and minister.

parson (PAR-suhn) A pastor or Protestant clergyman.

partisan strife (PAR-tuh-zuhn STRYF) Intense fighting between political parties.

patriot (PAY-tree-uht) A person who loves and defends his or her country.

pernicious (per-NIH-shuhs) Destructive, deadly, or wicked.

persecute (PUR-sih-kyoot) To attack or treat someone badly because of his or her beliefs.

politician (pah-luh-TIH-shun) A person who holds or runs for public office.

provoke (pruh-VOHK) To stir up feelings on purpose.

relinquish (rih-LIN-kwish) To give up, abandon, let go of, release, or to give over possession or control.

repugnant (rih-PUG-nuhnt) Exciting distaste or aversion—implies being against one's ideas, principles, or tastes and arousing resistance or hate.

righteousness (RY-chuhs-nes) The act or condition of doing what is just, good, or proper; goodness or morality.

shot heard 'round the world (SHOT HERD ROWND THUH WURLD) The first battle of the Revolution, at Concord, Massachusetts, April 19, 1775; from the last line of the first stanza of the "Concord Hymn"—a poem written by Ralph Waldo Emerson in 1886.

tannery (TA-nuh-ree) A place where animal skins are made into leather.

tyranny (TEER-uh-nee) A government in which one ruler has all the power.

tyrant (TY-ruhnt) A ruler who has all the power and uses it to hurt the people and country he rules.

vaccinate (VAK-suh-nayt) To give a person a shot to keep him or her from getting a particular disease.

vestry (VES-tree) Church council; the people elected to handle the business of an Anglican or Episcopal church.

void (VOYD) Empty; having no power.

Additional Resources

For more information about Patrick Henry, check out the following books and Web sites.

Books

Couvillon, Mark. *Patrick Henry's Virginia: A Guide to the Homes and Sites in the Life of an American Patriot*. Brookneal, VA: Patrick Henry Memorial Foundation, 2001.

Davis, Burke. *Three for Revolution*. New York: Harcourt Brace Jovanovitch, 1975.

Grote, Joann A. *Patrick Henry: American Statesman and Speaker*. New York: Chelsea House Publishers: 1999.

Sabin, Louis. *Patrick Henry: Voice of the American Revolution*. New York: Econo-Clad Books, 1999.

Web Sites

www.history.org
www.inmind.com/schools/lessons/PatrickHenry/index.html
www.pbs.org/ktca/liberty/
www.redhill.org

Bibliography

Henry, William Wirt. *Patrick Henry: Life, Correspondence, and Speeches*. 3 vols. New York: Charles Scribner's Sons, 1891.

Mayer, Henry. *A Son of Thunder: Patrick Henry and the American Republic.* Charlottesville: University Press of Virginia, 1991.

Mayo, Bernard. *Myths and Men: Patrick Henry, George Washington and Thomas Jefferson*. Athens, University of Georgia Press, 1959.

McCants, David A. *Patrick Henry the Orator.* New York: Greenwood Press, 1990.

McIlwaine, Henry Read, ed. *Official Letters of the Governors of the State of Virginia, Vol. 1*. Richmond: D. Bottom, 1926.

Meade, Robert Douthat. *Patrick Henry: Patriot in the Making.* Philadelphia: Lippincott, 1957.

Meade, Robert Douthat. *Patrick Henry: Practical Revolutionary.* Philadelphia: Lippincott, 1969.

State Historical Scoiety of Wisconsin. *Documentary History of the Ratification of the Constitution.* vol. VIII-X. Madison: State Historical Society of Wisconsin, 1988–1993.

Wirt, William. *Sketches of the Life and Character of Patrick Henry*. Philadelphia: James Webster, 1817 and many subsequent editions.

Index

About the Authors

Amy Kukla graduated from Roanoke College in 2000. Her interest in early American history and particularly Patrick Henry was invigorated when she moved to her father's house at Red Hill, Patrick Henry's last home and burial site near Brookneal, Virginia. "The more you learn about Patrick Henry," she says, "the more you realize he's a guy from history kids can really look up to. He's real hero material."

Dr. Jon Kukla graduated from Carthage College in 1970 and received his Ph.D. in history from the University of Toronto in 1980. He became director of the Patrick Henry Memorial Foundation in January 2000, after holding similar positions in New Orleans, Louisiana, and in Richmond, Virginia. Dr. Kukla is an expert on early American history, and is currently writing a narrative history about the Louisiana Purchase that will be published by Alfred A. Knopf in 2003.

Credits

Photo Credits

Pp. 4, 9, 27, 98 © Red Hill, The Patrick Henry National Memorial; pp. 6, 34, 49, 52-53, 58, 61, 66, 78 © courtesy of Map Division, The New York Public Library, Astor, Lenox and Tilden Foundations; p. 7 © Roger Tidman/CORBIS; pp. 10, 21, 23, 30, 44, 63, 69, 77 © Virginia Historical Society; p. 14 © Archive Photos; pp. 15, 17, 47, 64, 95 © The Library of Virginia; p. 16 © David Muench/CORBIS; p. 18 © Archivo Iconografico, S.A./CORBIS; pp. 28, 35, 38, 43, 56, 60, 74, 80, 82, 87, 88 © Bettmann/CORBIS; p. 31 © SuperStock; pp. 37, 90 © Lee Snider/CORBIS; p. 39 © Buddy Mays/CORBIS; p. 41 © Art Resource, NY; pp. 42, 48, 67, 71, 84, 94 © CORBIS; p. 55 © Hulton-Deutsch Collection/CORBIS; p. 70 © Burstein Collection/CORBIS; p. 83 © Joseph Sohm; Visions of America/CORBIS; p. 91 © North Wind Pictures; p. 93 © Bequest of Mrs. Benjamin Ogle Taylor; Collection of The Corcoran Gallery of Art/CORBIS.

Series Design

Laura Murawski

Layout Design

Corinne Jacob

Project Editor

Joanne Randolph